A NOTE TO PARENTS AND TEACHERS

Smithsonian Readers were created for children who are just starting on the amazing road to reading. These engaging books support the acquisition of reading skills, encourage children to learn about the world around them, and help to foster a lifelong love of books. These high-interest informational texts contain fascinating, real-world content designed to appeal to beginning readers. This early access to high-quality books provides an essential reading foundation that students will rely on throughout their school career.

The four levels in the Smithsonian Readers series target different stages of learning abilities. Each child is unique; age or grade level does not determine a particular reading level. See the inside back cover for complete descriptions of each reading level.

When sharing a book with beginning readers, read in short stretches, pausing often to talk about the pictures. Have younger children turn the pages and point to the pictures and familiar words. And be sure to reread favorite parts. As children become more independent readers, encourage them to share the ideas they are reading about and to discuss ideas and questions they have. Learning practice can be further extended with the quizzes after each title and the included fact cards.

There is no right or wrong way to share books with children. You are setting a pattern of enjoying and exploring books that will set a literacy foundation for their entire school career. Find time to read with your child, and pass on the amazing world of literacy.

Adria F. Klein, Ph.D.
Professor Emeritus
California State University San Bernardino

Smithsonian

READERS

Seriously Amazing

LEVEL 2

Nighttime Animals

Sea Life

Baby Animals

Dinosaurs

Solar System

Human Body

Silver Dolphin Books
An imprint of Printers Row Publishing Group
10350 Barnes Canyon Road, Suite 100, San Diego CA 92121
www.silverdolphinbooks.com

Printers Row Publishing Group is a division of Readerlink Distribution Services, LLC.
The Silver Dolphin Books name and logo are trademarks of Readerlink Distribution
Services, LLC.

ISBN 978-1-62686-452-8
Manufactured, printed, and assembled in Dongguan City, China
19 18 17 16 15   1 2 3 4 5

Nighttime Animals written by Brenda Scott Royce
Sea Life written by Emily Rose Oachs
Dinosaurs and Other Prehistoric Creatures written by Stephen Binns
Solar System and Human Body written by Ruth Strother
Baby Animals written by Courtney Acampora
Edited by Kaitlyn DiPerna
Editorial Assistance by Courtney Acampora
Cover Design by Jenna Riggs
Cover Production by Rusty von Dyl
Book Design by Kevin Plottner
Nighttime Animals, Baby Animals, Sea Life, and Human Body reviewed by
          Dr. Don E. Wilson, Curator Emeritus of the Department of Vertebrate
          Zoology, National Museum of Natural History, Smithsonian
Dinosaurs reviewed by Mike Brett-Surman, PhD, Museum Specialist for Fossil
          Dinosaurs, Reptiles, Amphibians, and Fish, National Museum of Natural
          History, Smithsonian
Solar System reviewed by Andrew K. Johnston, Geographer for the Center for Earth
          and Planetary Studies, National Air and Space Museum, Smithsonian

For Smithsonian Enterprises:
Kealy Gordon, Product Development Manager, Licensing
Ellen Nanney, Licensing Manager
Brigid Ferraro, Vice President, Education and Consumer Products
Carol LeBlanc, Senior Vice President, Education and Consumer Products
Chris Liedel, President

HOW TO USE THIS BOOK

Glossary

As you read each title, you will see words in **bold letters**. More information about these words can be found in the glossary at the end of each title.

Quizzes

Multiple-choice quizzes are included at the end of each title. Use these quizzes to check your understanding of the topic. Answers are printed at the end of the quiz, or you can reread the title to check your answers.

Fact Cards

Each title comes with six tear-out fact cards. Read the cards for fun or use them as quizzes with a friend or family member. You'll be impressed with all you can learn!

ABOUT THE SMITHSONIAN

Founded in 1846, the Smithsonian is the world's largest museum and research complex, consisting of 19 museums and galleries, the National Zoological Park, and nine research facilities. The Smithsonian's vision is to shape the future by preserving our heritage, discovering new knowledge, and sharing our resources with the world.

Kangaroo rats live in the desert.

They hide underground during the day, and come out at night when it is cooler.

Kangaroo rats use pouches on their cheeks to carry seeds back to their burrows.

These little rats hop upright on their back legs.

They use their long tails for balance, just like kangaroos!

Lying Low

Some animals are safer at night.

They come out after dark when there are fewer **predators** around.

A predator is an animal that eats another animal for food.

In the daytime, hedgehogs hide in holes or under piles of leaves.

At nighttime, they eat insects and small animals.

Short, sharp spines on the hedgehog's body are extra protection.

The opossum stays out of sight during the day. At night it searches for food.

Opossums sometimes look for food in backyards, gardens, and garbage cans.

When an opossum is really scared, it will play dead!

Nighttime Hunters

For a tiger, nighttime is the best time to hunt.

A tiger's stripes help it blend in with the shadows of the dark forest.

predator and prey

A tiger may travel several miles in a single night tracking its **prey**.

Prey is an animal that is eaten by another animal for food.

Alligators can remain still for hours, waiting for prey to come near.

An alligator drifting in the water looks like a log.

This helps it sneak up on its prey.

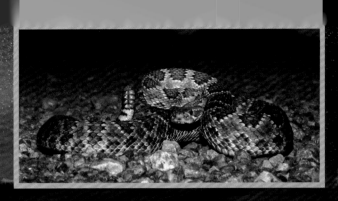

Rattlesnakes are excellent night hunters.

But they cannot see well in the dark.

Rattlesnakes have heat-sensing pits on each side of their heads.

These pits sense the body heat of rodents and other animals.

moth

The whippoorwill loves to eat moths.

Moths come out at night, so that is when the whippoorwill goes hunting.

This small bird flies with its mouth wide open to catch moths and other bugs.

Midnight Snackers

The hippopotamus is big and powerful. It doesn't have to hide from predators.

During the day, a hippo sleeps in the water.

At night, it comes ashore to eat grass and plants.

Some creatures come out at night when there is less **competition** for food.

The black-crowned night heron fishes at night, when larger herons are asleep.

moth

Moths and butterflies are a lot alike.

Moths and butterflies are both winged insects that drink nectar from flowers.

Butterflies are daytime creatures.

Moths come out at night.

This way, there are enough flowers to go around.

Big Eyes

Special eyes help night creatures see in the dark.

The tarsier is a tiny animal with enormous eyes.

Each of the tarsier's eyes is larger than its brain!

The tarsier's big eyes help it see in the dark.

Tarsiers spend most of their time in the trees, like their monkey relatives.

At night, they search for their favorite food—insects.

Ocelots have a special layer in their eyes that helps them see in the dark.

Ocelots hunt for mice, rats, and other small animals at night.

These wild cats are great climbers and strong swimmers.

Tree frogs need good vision so they can leap from branch to branch in the dark.

Awesome Ears

Large ears help nighttime animals hear well. The bat-eared fox points its enormous ears toward the ground to listen for sounds made by insects. When it hears insects below the ground, the fox starts digging.

Termites are the bat-eared fox's favorite food.

One bat-eared fox can eat more than a million termites in a single year!

termites

Jackrabbits have very good hearing.

Their big ears help jackrabbits hear approaching predators.

Tap, tap, tap. The aye-aye taps on a tree branch…then listens carefully.

The aye-aye uses his big ears to tell if the branch has a hole.

The aye-aye knows that insects hide in tree holes.

The aye-aye uses its long finger to pry a bug out of its hiding place.

Super Noses

A good sense of smell helps nighttime animals find food, stay away from danger, and find friends in the dark.

The two-toed sloth has a very good sense of smell.

This slow-moving animal lives high up in the trees and mainly eats leaves.

Most night birds have good eyesight, but the kiwi does not.

The kiwi uses its excellent sense of smell to find food.

The kiwi uses nostrils on the tip of its beak to find worms underground.

The Baird's tapir uses its long nose to search for food at night.

Moths don't have noses but they do have a good sense of smell.

Their antennae work like noses to detect smells.

Some flowers bloom only at night, when bees and butterflies are resting.

These flowers need moths and bats to spread their **pollen**.

The sweet smell of evening primrose attracts moths.

Whiskers and Webs

The sense of touch is very important to nighttime animals.

Many nighttime animals have long, thick whiskers on their faces.

Whiskers help nighttime animals find their way in the dark.

The leopard's long, thick whiskers are very sensitive.

Whiskers help the leopard find food and keep the leopard from bumping into things in the dark!

Black widow spiders build webs of strong silk.

At night, the female black widow sits in the center of her web.

She waits for an insect to get tangled in the silky strands.

When an insect enters the web, the silk threads shake.

The shaking tells the black widow that she has trapped her next meal.

Night Flight

Many types of birds migrate, or travel long distances, at certain times of the year.

Most migrating birds fly at night.

At night, the air is cooler and calmer, and there are fewer predators.

How do birds find their way in the dark?

They use the moon and stars to guide them!

The patterns formed by stars are like maps in the sky for migrating birds.

Songbirds make many sounds while migrating.

Their songs help them stick together in the dark and warn other birds about danger.

Fireflies light up the night sky.

Fireflies bellies have a built-in light source.

Fireflies flash their lights to locate each

Bats may have the best hearing of all the animals.

The large pointed ears of the Virginia big-eared bat look like funnels and help gather sound.

Bats can hear high-pitched noises that people cannot hear.

Bats find insects and other objects in the dark using **echolocation**.

They send out high-pitched sounds.

The sounds bounce off nearby objects.

The bat can identify the object and where it is by the sound of its echo.

Owls

Owls hunt for mice and other small animals at night.

Owls' curved wings and soft feathers let them fly without making a sound.

Swooping down silently, they catch prey by surprise.

Owls' super-sized eyes are made for night hunting.

Owls can't move their eyes in their sockets as people do.

Instead they rotate their heads to see around them.

Like many
night owls,
the barn owl has
mismatched ears!

One ear is bigger, and one is smaller.

One ear is higher on the owl's head
than the other.

This helps the owl quickly pinpoint the
source of sounds.

Then barn owls can catch their prey in
total darkness.

Night Noises

noisy tokay gecko

Nighttime animals can be very noisy.

Owls hoot, coyotes howl, frogs croak, and crickets chirp.

In the dark, animals make sounds to find friends or frighten enemies.

croaking bullfrog

Coyote families
are called packs.

At night, the packs
hunt together.

Coyote packs
howl to say: "This
is our space."

Daytime Sleepers

When the sun rises, nighttime animals look for a safe place to sleep.

Some find shelter underground. Others prefer the trees.

Some hide under bushes or in tall grass.

Sugar gliders nest in trees.

Up to twelve sugar gliders may share one nest.

A two-toed sloth sleeps between the branches of a tree.

Its brown hair helps it blend in.

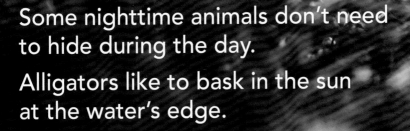

Some nighttime animals don't need to hide during the day.

Alligators like to bask in the sun at the water's edge.

Leopards have excellent balance.

These large cats can sleep on tree branches without falling off.

By the time the sun is high up in the sky, most nighttime animals are fast asleep.

When darkness falls, they'll come out again, to eat, hunt, travel, and play.

NIGHTTIME ANIMALS
QUIZ

1. What are animals that are active at night called?

a) Mammals

b) Nocturnal

c) Special

2. Where do hippopotamuses sleep during the day?

a) In a tree

b) In the grass

c) In the water

3. Which animal has eyes larger than its brain?

a) Tarsier

b) Bat-eared fox

c) Kiwi

4. What is a bat-eared fox's favorite food?

a) Fruit

b) Grass

c) Termites

5. Which insect lights up the night sky?

a) Firefly

b) Termite

c) Black widow spider

6. How do bats find insects and other objects in the dark?

a) Scent

b) Touch

c) Echolocation

GLOSSARY

Burrows: holes or tunnels dug in the ground by an animal for shelter

Competition: the act of two or more kinds of animals looking for the same resource such as food or territory

Echolocation: a method bats use to find objects using sound waves

Nocturnal: active at night

Pollen: powder on a flower that when moved to a different flower, helps make a new flower

Predators: animals that hunt other animals for food

Prey: an animal that is hunted by other animals for food

Smithsonian

SEA LIFE

Emily Rose Oachs

CONTENTS

The Earth's Oceans

The Earth's oceans are vast and deep.

They cover two-thirds of the planet.

Earth's salty waters are divided into five different oceans.

Arctic

Pacific

Indian

Atlantic

Southern (or Antarctic)

The oceans are very important to life on Earth.

Many different kinds of animals call the ocean home.

Marine Mollusks

Mollusks are soft-bodied creatures.

Some mollusks grow hard outer shells.

Other mollusks have no shell at all.

Oysters, sea slugs, snails, squids, and octopuses are all mollusks!

Snails move using a big, flat muscle called a "foot."

The foot slowly drags them from place to place.

Giant clams are Earth's biggest mollusks.

Their shells may be more than four feet across.

They can weigh more than five hundred pounds!

Octopuses have round, soft bodies.

They can fit into tight spaces.

A fifty-pound octopus can squeeze through a two-inch hole!

Spiny Sea Urchins and Sea Stars

Sea urchins and sea stars live on the ocean floor.

They don't have eyes or brains.

Water flows through their bodies instead of blood.

Sea urchins look like spiny balls.

Sea urchins use their spines to walk and eat.

Sometimes the spines are poisonous!

Sea stars are bright colors, such as orange, blue, or purple.

They may have as many as twenty-four arms!

Sometimes a sea star loses an arm to protect itself.

A new arm will grow back in its place.

Each arm has tiny tube feet.

These tube feet help sea stars crawl and stick to surfaces.

Stinging Jellyfish

Jellyfish have bell-shaped, see-through bodies. They have long, stinging **tentacles**. Tentacles are flexible, arm-like body parts.

Jellyfish are mostly made up of water.

They do not have brains, hearts, bones, or blood.

Most jellyfish can't swim, so they float through the ocean.

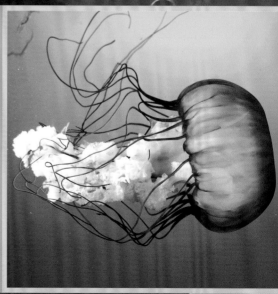

The lion's mane jellyfish is the longest animal in the world.

Its tentacles can grow to over one hundred feet!

Jellyfish use their tentacles to catch and kill food.

Box jellyfish have cube-shaped bells, or bodies.

Long tentacles grow from each of the bell's corners.

A box jellyfish's sting could kill a person.

Colorful Coral and Coral Reefs

Coral can be all different shapes, sizes, and colors.

Some corals are hard and rigid, and others are soft and flexible.

They can look like brains, feathers, or even broccoli!

Corals have tube-shaped bodies.

One end of the body attaches to a hard surface.

The other end has a mouth and stinging tentacles.

Corals live in groups, or **colonies**.

Corals die and leave their hard skeletons behind.

Over time, these skeletons build up into a coral reef.

It takes thousands of years for a coral reef to form!

Coral reefs are an important home for sea animals.

Sea horses, sharks, and other fish swim through coral reefs.

Sea Turtles: Long Distance Swimmers

Sea turtles have a hard shell and paddle-like flippers.

Sea turtles use their front flippers to swim through the ocean.

They use their back flippers to steer.

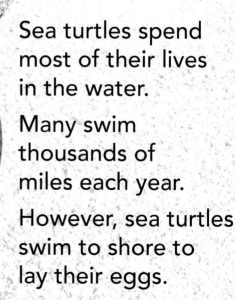

Sea turtles spend most of their lives in the water.

Many swim thousands of miles each year.

However, sea turtles swim to shore to lay their eggs.

Leatherback sea turtles don't have a hard shell.

Leatherback sea turtles have flexible, leathery shells.

They eat jellyfish, sea urchins, and squid.

Green sea turtles can swim underwater for a long time.

They can hold their breath for five hours!

Sea Anemones and Clown Fish: Ocean Friends

Sea anemones are colorful creatures.

They have soft bodies and stinging tentacles.

They attach themselves to rocks or coral reefs.

Clown fish are bright orange with white stripes.

Clown fish and sea anemones live together in the coral reef.

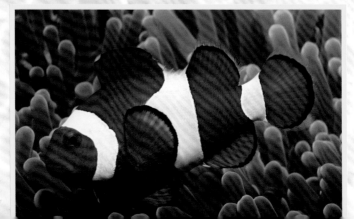

Sea anemones protect clown fish.

Their stinging tentacles keep clown fish **predators** away.

But clown fish are safe from a sea anemone's sting.

A special mucus covers the bodies of clown fish.

Clown fish help to keep their sea anemones clean.

They snack on sea anemones' leftovers.

Incredible Fish

Fish are animals that live in water.

Their bodies are covered in scales.

Fish use fins to swim through the water.

They use **gills** to breathe.

Fish come in many shapes, sizes, and colors.

Sharks, puffer fish, and leafy sea dragons are all fish!

Sea horses are tiny fish with tiny fins.

They curl their tails around sea grasses.

This keeps them from floating away!

Sailfish have long, sword-like noses.

They are the ocean's fastest fish.

They leap out of the ocean at almost seventy miles per hour!

Sharks: Fierce Fish

Many sharks are fierce fish.

Hundreds of sharp teeth may line their mouths.

Sharks live throughout the ocean, from its depths to shallow coastal waters.

Sharks' skeletons are made of **cartilage** instead of bones.

Cartilage is a strong, flexible tissue.

A human's nose and ears are made of cartilage.

Great white sharks' mouths have three hundred razor-sharp teeth.

Their powerful bite quickly kills their large **prey**.

Tiger sharks are violent, fierce ocean predators.

Their curved teeth rip through the shells of sea turtles.

Nurse sharks swim slowly through the coral reefs.

They eat fish, shrimp, and crabs from the ocean floor.

Rays: Flat Fish

Rays have flat, circular bodies.

Their fins spread like wings from their bodies.

Some rays have a sharp spine on their tail.

Manta rays move by flapping their fins like wings.

Sometimes they leap out of the water!

Stingrays often rest on the ocean floor.

Sand partly covers their bodies.

This hides them from predators.

Electric rays have special organs.

These organs produce electrical shocks!

Electric rays use the shocks for **defense** and catching prey.

Life in the Deep Sea

In some places, the ocean floor is miles beneath the water's surface.

These are the deepest parts of the ocean.

There the world is cold and dark.
But many sea creatures still live there.

Fangtooth fish have sharp teeth and poor eyesight.

They swim around until they bump into prey.

Animals in the deep sea rarely see daylight.
Some deep sea animals create their own light.

Anglerfish have a long spine on their head.
The tip of the spine lights up.
The spine is like a fishing pole.
Its light attracts prey to the anglerfish.

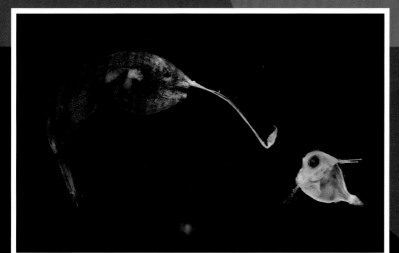

Dolphins and Porpoises: Breathing with Blowholes

Dolphins and porpoises are mammals that live in the ocean.

Mammals can't breathe underwater.

They must swim to the ocean's surface to breathe.

Dolphins and porpoises breathe using **blowholes**.

Blowholes are nostrils on top of their head.

Porpoises are speedy swimmers.

They have thicker bodies than dolphins.

Porpoises also have blunter noses and smaller mouths than dolphins do.

Dolphins make noises to talk to other dolphins.

They whistle, click, chirp, and slap their tails.

These mean they are happy, sad, scared, or want to play.

Whales: The Ocean's Largest

Like dolphins and porpoises, whales are mammals that live in the ocean.

Whales' bodies have a thick layer of fat, called **blubber**.

Blubber keeps them warm in cold waters.

Whales are some of the largest animals in the ocean.

Blue whales are the biggest animals on Earth. Their tongues are as heavy as an elephant!

Orcas are fierce hunters.

Their four-inch-long teeth slice through their prey.

Orcas hunt and travel in groups called **pods**.

Humpback whales make low, song-like noises in the ocean.

These whales may sing for hours.

They use the songs to talk to other humpback whales.

Flying, Floating, and Diving: Sea Birds

Some birds also make their home by the sea.

They fly above it, float on it, and dive in it.

These birds rely on the ocean for survival.

Pelicans use a pouch under their bill to catch fish.

They scoop up fish in the pouch.

Then they drain the water and swallow the fish whole.

Oystercatchers wade along the ocean coasts.

They use their strong, flat bill to open mollusk shells.

Penguins huddle together on the ice in the Antarctic Ocean.

Penguins can't fly, but they are excellent swimmers.

Sometimes penguins slide across the ice on their bellies!

SEA LIFE QUIZ

1. The Earth's oceans cover how much of the planet?

a) One-fourth

b) Two-thirds

c) One-half

2. How long does it take for a coral reef to form?

a) Thousands of years

b) One week

c) One day

3. Which ocean creature helps protect clown fish?

a) Sea star

b) Sea urchin

c) Sea anemone

4. What do fish use to breathe?
a) Nose
b) Tail
c) Gills

5. Which animal is a mammal?
a) Dolphin
b) Shark
c) Jellyfish

6. Which animals use songs to talk to each other?
a) Penguins
b) Humpback whales
c) Great white sharks

Answers: 1) b 2) a 3) c 4) c 5) a 6) b

GLOSSARY

Blowholes: holes on the top of the heads of some ocean mammals used for breathing

Blubber: a layer of fat

Cartilage: a tough, flexible material

Colonies: groups of coral growing together

Defense: protecting against attack

Gills: organs on fish that let them get oxygen from the water to breathe

Pods: groups of whales

 **Predators:** animals that kill and eat other animals

Prey: an animal that is hunted or killed by another animal for food

Tentacles: flexible, arm-like body parts that are used for grabbing and moving

DINOSAURS
AND OTHER
PREHISTORIC CREATURES

Stephen Binns

CONTENTS

What's in a Name?

Dino is based on a Greek word for "fearfully great." *Saur* is a Greek word for "lizard."

Dinosaur means "fearfully great lizard."

But not all dinosaurs should be feared. And one more thing: These "lizards" were not true lizards!

Father of the Dinosaur

The name "dinosaur" was created by an English scientist, Sir Richard Owen.

Sir Richard was a dinosaur scientist, or **paleontologist**.

He knew that dinosaurs were not lizards.

No one knows why Sir Richard called them "fearfully great lizards."

Paleontologists have solved many mysteries about dinosaurs.

No one has ever solved this one!

Dinosaurs vs. Lizards

Dinosaurs are **reptiles**.

Lizards are reptiles.

But you can see a difference between the two.

Lizards stand with their legs sprawled out.

But, dinosaurs stood on straight legs.

A modern reptile is an animal with dry, scaly skin.

Modern reptiles have no hair.

Most reptiles lay eggs.

All reptiles have lungs for breathing air.

Most reptiles today are "cold-blooded."

What Else Is Not a Dinosaur?

Pterosaurs were flying reptiles.
But they were not flying dinosaurs.

Pterosaurs had light, hollow bones, like birds.

The smallest pterosaurs were as small as a sparrow.

The largest had wings that stretched as wide as the wings of a small plane.

At the end of the dinosaur age, mosasaurs ruled the seas.

Mosasaurs were true *saurs*.

They were swimming lizards.

They had flippers instead of sprawling legs.

Some were fifty feet long — twice as long as a great white shark!

All in the Hips

Paleontologists have discovered more than twelve hundred types of dinosaurs.

These types are put into individual **species**.

Paleontologists put all of the species into two groups.

There were lizard-hipped dinosaurs — the Saurischia (saw-riss-KEY-uh).

And there were bird-hipped dinosaurs — the Ornithischia (or-nih-THISS-key-uh).

Tyrannosaurus rex stood on two legs.

Apatosaurus stood on four legs.

But both of them were lizard-hipped dinosaurs.

Stegosaurus was the size of a school bus.

It certainly does not look like a bird.

But *Stegosaurus* was a bird-hipped dinosaur!

Dinosaurs Among Us

Paleontologists believe that some of the saurischian dinosaurs **evolved** into living animals.

They changed very slowly to become animals we see every day — birds!

But birds did not evolve from bird-hipped dinosaurs.

They evolved from lizard-hipped dinosaurs.

And lizards did not evolve from any kind of dinosaur.

Lizards were around long before the dinosaurs.

Some paleontologists never speak of the dinosaurs as dead.

As they see it, the dinosaurs are still here.

Have you ever woken up to the song of a bird?

Some paleontologists wake up to the singing of dinosaurs!

What's Wrong with This Picture?

Here is a picture of a pink dinosaur with black stripes.

Maybe you are thinking, "Dinosaurs were not pink with black stripes."

Maybe you're right. Who knows?

Dinosaurs have left us **fossils**.

We find their bones, their teeth, and their footprints.

We even find the patterns of their skin pressed into stone.

But dinosaur color is mostly a mystery.

So why not a pink-and-black-striped dinosaur?

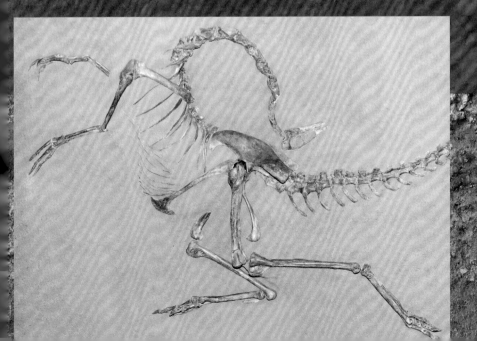

Family Life

Look at these fossil footprints.
What do you see?

A paleontologist might see an adult dinosaur walking with its babies.

This can tell the paleontologist that some dinosaurs lived in families.

One way to study dinosaur families is to watch the way birds act.

Birds are pretty good parents.

Some dinosaurs were probably good parents, too.

Dinosaur Dining

Some dinosaurs were **carnivores**.

Some dinosaurs were **herbivores**.

Carnivores eat other animals.

Herbivores eat plants (including herbs).

To learn what dinosaurs ate, paleontologists can study their tooth fossils.

Here are two types of dinosaur teeth.

One is the tooth of a carnivore.

One shows the teeth of a herbivore.

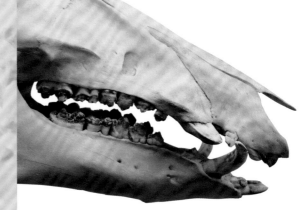

Can you tell which is which?

Meet a Meat Eater...
and Some
Gentler Giants

This is the tooth of an *Allosaurus*, a fearsome carnivore.

The tooth is pointed and curved, like a pirate's sword.

It has zigzag edges, like a steak knife does for cutting meat.

This is the tooth of a plant-eating *Edmontonia*.

The tooth is flat.

Rows of flat teeth are better for grinding plants.

There are other ways to learn what dinosaurs ate.

One way is to look at living animals.

This giraffe has a long neck to feed on the highest leaves of trees.

What do you think *this* herbivore ate?

Total Strangers

This is a "duckbill" herbivore named *Corythosaurus*.

This is a horned carnivore named *Ceratosaurus*.

Both dinosaurs lived in North America.

But these two dinosaurs never met.

Ceratosaurus died tens of millions of years before *Corythosaurus* came along.

Ceratosaurus is more ancient to *Corythosaurus* than *Corythosaurus* is to us today!

The two dinosaurs would be strangers to each other.

And they're pretty strange to paleontologists, too!

No one knows why *Ceratosaurus* had that stubby horn.

Some think that *Corythosaurus* blew air through its helmet-head to make unique sounds.

So one dinosaur had a strange horn on its head.

And one dinosaur honked its strange head like a horn!

95

End of an Era

Where did the last of the dinosaurs go?

Would you believe that they were killed by an invader from outer space?

Most scientists believe this.

A giant **asteroid** from outer space crashed into the Earth sixty-six million years ago.

It left a hole, or crater, about a hundred miles wide.

The crash of the giant space rock sent up a cloud of rock dust.

The dust darkened Earth's skies.

Most plants and animals died.

Many dinosaurs may have died right away —
in fires,

floods, and earthquakes caused by the crash.

Others may have died away slowly, in a world that was no longer theirs.

How to Become a Fossil

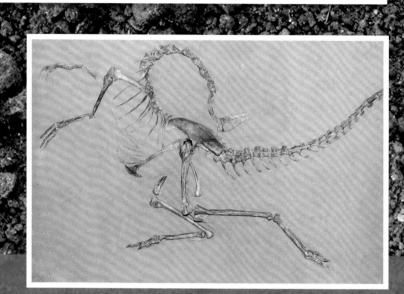

The trick to becoming a fossil is to get buried in a hurry.

Most fossil bones are from creatures that died in or near water.

The water quickly carried mud or sand over the bones.

The mud or sand hardened into stone.

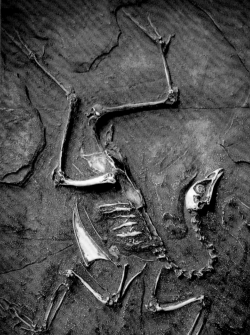

But most bones do not end up like that.

A creature dies and the body is eaten or weathered away. Paleontologists say that only one bone in a billion becomes a fossil.

There are now seven billion people on Earth. Every human has two hundred and six bones.

Imagine a future paleontologist collecting the fossils from all of us.

That paleontologist might end up with just one bag of bones!

Life Goes On

But we keep finding fossils. This is a very good thing!

There is still so much to be learned.

For example:

When the dinosaurs died, little creatures from our own family, **mammals**, lived on.

Why?

Did their warm blood help them with the skies grew dark?

Or their small size? Did they hide in holes in the ground?

Most of the dinosaurs died but lizards are still here.

Why?

Crocodiles and snakes and turtles and frogs and fish and birds are still here.

Why?

And you're here, of course, thanks to those little mammals.

It's up to you to figure out why we are here!

DINOSAURS QUIZ

1. What does the Greek word "saur" mean?
a) Great
b) Lizard
c) Reptile

2. What is the name for a dinosaur scientist?
a) Paleontologist
b) Pathologist
c) Herbivore

3. Which was a flying reptile?
a) Mosasaur
b) Pterosaur
c) Saurischia

4. What were bird-hipped dinosaurs called?
a) Apatosaurus
b) Saurischia
c) Ornithischia

5. Which animals are relatives of dinosaurs?
a) Mammals
b) Birds
c) Snakes

6. What do herbivores eat?
a) Meat
b) Prey
c) Plants

GLOSSARY

Asteroid: rock in space; they can be as small as a boulder or as big as a country

Carnivores: meat eaters

Evolved: changed very slowly to become something new

 **Fossils:** the remains of prehistoric life found in stone or evidence of life from the geologic past

Herbivores: plant eaters

Mammals: animals that have hair, "warm blood," and nurse their young with milk

Paleontologist: (pay-lee-on-TOL-oh-jist) scientist who studies fossils

 **Reptiles:** "cold-blooded" animals with scaly skin

Species: a group of living things different from all other groups

Smithsonian

SOLAR
SYSTEM

Ruth Strother

CONTENTS

The Solar System

A solar system is a star and the planets, planets' moons, and other space objects that move around the star.

Our solar system moves around one star that we call the Sun.

There are probably billions of other solar systems in the universe!

Stars and Sun

Stars are huge
burning balls of gas.
We can see thousands of stars in the
night sky. But only one star is in our
solar system. That star is the Sun.

The Sun is made of gas and dust. The Sun is huge! It makes up more than ninety-nine percent of the mass (or stuff) in our solar system. All other space objects in our solar system were made from the stuff that didn't get pulled into the Sun when it formed.

Gravity and Orbit

Gravity causes an object to pull other objects toward it. The force of the pull depends on the object's size. The Sun is huge, so its gravity is strong. All other objects in the solar system are pulled toward the Sun.

The Sun's gravity pulls space objects into a path. The path leads them around the Sun. This path is called an orbit.

Moons are a little different.

Moons orbit a planet. So a moon orbits its planet while the planet orbits the Sun.

Galaxy

The solar system is one small part of a galaxy. Galaxies are made of dust, gas, and billions of stars. Billions of galaxies spin in outer space. Some galaxies gather in a huge group like stars gather into galaxies.

Our galaxy has hundreds of billions of stars! From Earth, all those stars look a bit like a path of spilled milk. Our galaxy is called the Milky Way.

Mercury

Mercury is the closest planet to the Sun. Mercury is hard for us to see. It is hidden by the Sun's glare. Mercury has a thin **atmosphere**. There is very little air or other gases on Mercury. The sky is always black.

Mercury is a dry, rocky planet. It has huge cliffs and holes called **craters**. Mercury is freezing cold at night. But in the day, Mercury is very hot.

A day on Mercury lasts more than fifty-eight days on Earth.

Venus

Venus is the second planet from the Sun. And Venus is the closest planet to Earth. Venus and Earth are about the same size. Some people call them sisters or twins.

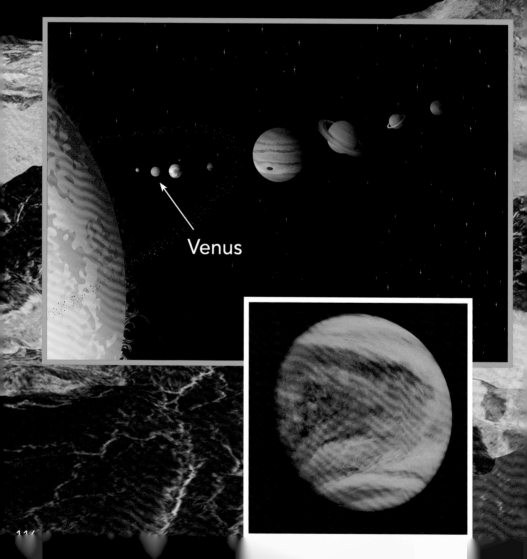

Venus

It is scorching hot on Venus. The air is full of deadly acid. The sky is yellow with strange clouds and lightning.

A day on Venus lasts more than two hundred days on Earth.

Earth

Earth

Earth is the
third planet
from the
Sun. Earth is
the only planet
with liquid water
on its surface. Most of Earth's surface is
covered with water. It even looks blue
when seen from space!

Earth has the right mix of air, water, and warmth from the Sun. This mix makes life possible. Earth is home to more than thirty million different forms of life.

Mars

Mars is the fourth planet from the Sun. Its soil is filled with iron. The iron rusts because of the Martian air. The rust makes the soil look red. The red color gives Mars its nickname, the Red Planet.

Mars may have once looked more like Earth. It even has water deep in the ground. People want to explore Mars to understand how the planet changed.

A day on Mars lasts almost as long as a day on Earth.

Jupiter

Jupiter is the fifth planet from the Sun. It is one of the gas giants. Jupiter is the biggest planet in the solar system. And Jupiter has the most moons. So far, **scientists** have found sixty-seven moons orbiting Jupiter.

Jupiter

A huge storm has been whirling on Jupiter for hundreds of years. The storm is called the Great Red Spot. The Great Red Spot is as big as Earth. It used to be even bigger!

A day on Jupiter lasts about ten hours.

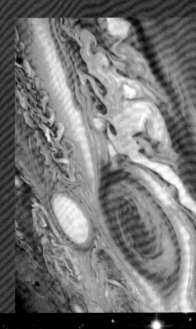

Saturn

Saturn

Saturn is the sixth planet from the Sun. Saturn is famous for its seven beautiful rings. The rings are made of ice, dust, and billions of

rock pieces. Some pieces are the size of tiny icy grains. Some pieces are as big as mountains!

Something strange happens about every fourteen years. Saturn's rings seem to disappear. That's because Saturn becomes tilted. When the rings' edges face Earth, we can't see them.

A day on Saturn lasts just over ten hours.

Uranus

Uranus is the seventh planet from the Sun. You need a **telescope** to see Uranus. Uranus looks like a green pea through a telescope. The green color comes from the gas in Uranus's atmosphere.

Uranus

Uranus is a gas giant. Some of the gas that covers Uranus is icy. So Uranus is also called the ice giant. Uranus is the coldest planet in our solar system.

A day on Uranus lasts almost eighteen hours.

Neptune

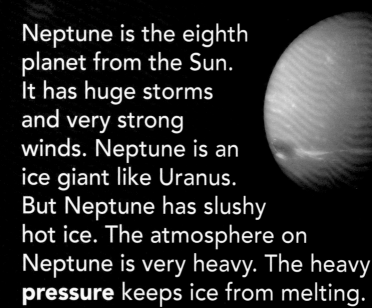

Neptune

Neptune is the eighth
planet from the Sun.
It has huge storms
and very strong
winds. Neptune is an
ice giant like Uranus.
But Neptune has slushy
hot ice. The atmosphere on
Neptune is very heavy. The heavy
pressure keeps ice from melting.

The pressure is even heavier deep inside Neptune. Some scientists think the gas deep inside is being squeezed into diamonds!

A day on Neptune lasts about sixteen hours.

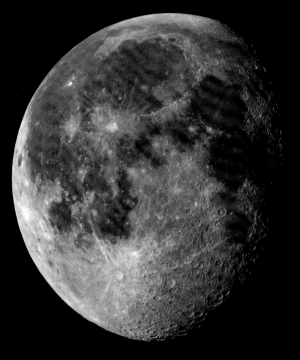

Moons are space objects. Each moon orbits a planet. The planet's gravity keeps a moon on its path.

Some planets have many moons. Some planets have no moon at all.

Jupiter has more moons than any other planet. Jupiter has sixty-seven moons.

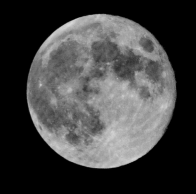

Earth has one moon. We on Earth see just one side of the Moon. Only **astronauts** in space have seen the other side of the Moon.

Asteroids, Comets, and Meteoroids

Asteroids are large rocks that orbit the Sun. Comets orbit the Sun too. Comets are like dirty snowballs in space. They are dust and rocks trapped in frozen liquid. Meteoroids are made of rocks and metals.

Sometimes meteoroids enter Earth's atmosphere. They heat up and glow. Then they are called meteors. When you wish upon a falling star, you're wishing upon a meteor!

If the meteor hits Earth, it's called a meteorite. Some meteorites leave craters.

SOLAR SYSTEM QUIZ

1. How many stars are in our solar system?
a) Billions and billions
b) Thousands
c) One

2. What do moons orbit?
a) The Sun
b) A planet
c) The Solar System

3. Which planet is sometimes called Earth's sister or twin?
a) Venus
b) Mars
c) Mercury

4. Which planet has more moons than any other planet?

a) Saturn

b) Uranus

c) Jupiter

5. What is the Great Red Spot?

a) A huge storm

b) A massive crater

c) A giant cloud

6. What are Saturn's rings made of?

a) Gases and colorful clouds

b) Comets and asteroids

c) Ice, dust, and rock pieces

GLOSSARY

Astronauts: people who are trained to travel into outer space

Atmosphere: the gases surrounding a planet or moon

Craters: large dents on the surface of a planet or moon made by a meteorite

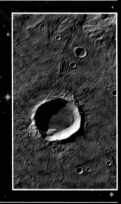

Pressure: the ongoing force from one object pushing or pressing against another object

Scientists: people who are experts in science

Telescope: a tool that makes distant objects look closer and bigger

Smithsonian

BABY ANIMALS

Courtney Acampora

CONTENTS

Baby Animals

Baby animals come in all shapes and sizes.

Some are small and some are big.

Baby animals can have feathers, soft fur, or no hair at all!

Some babies stay with their mothers their whole lives.

Baby animals follow their mothers to learn about the world.

Lions

Cozy Koalas

Koalas are not bears.

Koalas are **marsupials**.

Marsupials are animals that have pouches.

Marsupial mothers carry their young in their pouches.

Baby koalas are called joeys.

Joeys are the size of a jellybean when they are born!

Joeys crawl into their mother's pouch to grow.

Joeys drink their mother's milk in the pouch.

Joeys leave the pouch when they are seven months old.

Then they ride on their mother's back.

At one year old, joeys can climb trees and eat leaves.

Big Baby Elephants

A baby elephant is called a calf.
Elephant calves are some of the biggest babies on Earth!

When they are born, they are three feet tall and weigh two hundred pounds!

Baby elephants are part of a **herd**.

A herd is a group of female elephants and their calves.

A herd protects the babies.

Baby elephants drink their mother's milk.

When they are two or three years old, they eat grass.

They use their trunks to grab the grass.

Male calves stay with their mothers until they are teenagers.

Female calves stay with their mothers their whole lives.

Part of the Troop: Gorilla Babies

A baby gorilla only weighs four pounds at birth.

The baby's mother carries it against her chest.

When it is older, the baby rides on its mother's back through the forest.

Gorillas are **mammals**.

Mammals are warm-blooded, produce milk, and give birth to live young.

Baby gorillas learn to walk when they are five months old.

Baby gorillas like to climb on trees!

Their mother builds a nest of leaves to sleep in every night.

Baby gorillas share a nest with their mother.

A Lion's Pride and Joy

A baby lion is called a cub.
Cubs live in a **pride**.
A pride is a group of lions.

Mother lions give birth to three or four babies at a time.

Cubs sleep and play with their mother and other cubs.

Cubs start hunting at eleven months old.

Male cubs start growing a mane at one year old.

A mane is the long hair that grows around their head.

Pandas: Bamboo Babies

Baby pandas are very small when they are born.

They are pink, hairless, and blind.

Panda cubs depend on their mothers.

Baby pandas are helpless for their first three months.

The mother panda holds the baby in her paw.

She holds the baby panda close.

Baby pandas grow and play with their mother.

Baby pandas eat bamboo when they are seven months old.

Bamboo is their favorite food.

Tiny Turtles

Baby turtles are **reptiles**.

Reptiles are cold-blooded, don't have hair, and lay eggs.

Snakes, lizards, and crocodiles are reptiles too.

snake   lizard   crocodile

A mother turtle digs a nest on a beach.

She lays her eggs and covers the nest with sand.

Then she goes back to the ocean.

In about sixty days, baby turtles break through their shells.

They crawl out of their nest and head to the ocean.

In the ocean, they find food and grow strong.

Cuddly Bear Cubs

Baby brown bears are called cubs.

Cubs are born in January and February.

Cubs are born in a **den**.

A den is a place for animals to rest during winter.

Two cubs are born at one time.

Cubs are born without hair and teeth.

They snuggle against their mother's fur to keep warm.

Cubs follow their mother out of the den in the spring.

Darling Dolphins

A baby dolphin is called a calf.
A mother dolphin has one calf at a time.
Sometimes, a mother dolphin has twins.

A dolphin is a mammal.

An ocean mammal must come up to the surface to breathe.

The mother dolphin takes the calf to the surface for its first breath.

The calf drinks its mother's milk for up to two years.

It learns to swim by staying close to its mother.

It learns to play by chasing other dolphins and tossing seaweed.

A calf stays with its mother for up to eight years.

Nesting Owl Chicks

An owl is a bird.

Birds have feathers, lay eggs, and most can fly.

A baby owl is called a chick.

The mother owl lays eggs in a nest.

The mother sits on the eggs to keep them warm.

The chicks hatch from their eggs!
Their mother protects and feeds
the chicks in the nest.

Owls are **nocturnal**.
Nocturnal means awake and active
at night.
Chicks learn to hunt and fly at night.

Giraffes Standing Tall

A baby giraffe is called a calf.

A baby giraffe learns to walk when it's only one hour old!

A calf drinks its mother's milk.

When a calf is four months old it eats leaves.

The calf joins other babies.

They learn to play together.

One of the mothers watches the calves so they are protected from **predators**.

A predator is an animal that kills and eats other animals for food.

Predators

Playful Pups: Sea Otters

Sea otters are playful animals.

They like to wrestle and chase their tail.

Baby sea otters are called pups.

Sea otter pups have special hair that helps them float in the water.

At first, a pup cannot swim.

The pup floats on its mother's belly.

The mother otter dives down to get food for the pup.

The pup floats at the surface wrapped in kelp.

After two months, the pup learns to swim on its own.

Spotted Babies: Cheetahs

Baby cheetahs are called cubs.

A mother cheetah usually gives birth to three to five cubs at one time.

Cubs are born wit spots on their fur.

The spots **camouflage** the cubs in the grass.

Camouflage helps animals hide and blend in.

Their mother moves the cubs every few days.

The cubs are moved so they are protected from predators.

The cubs live with their mother for two years.

Their mother teaches them how to hunt and play.

Hold on Tight, Baby Chimpanzee!

Chimpanzees are a type of ape.

An ape is a mammal similar to a monkey, but without a tail.

Chimpanzees are closely related to humans.

Baby chimpanzees are born with pink skin and dark hair.

Baby chimpanzees have a white tail tuft.

When they get older, the tail tuft disappears.

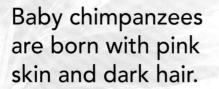

Baby chimpanzees hold onto their mothers' bellies.

They also ride on their mothers' backs like a piggyback ride!

Baby chimpanzees drink their mother's milk until they are three years old.

They live with their mothers for up to ten years.

BABY ANIMALS QUIZ

1. What are marsupials?
a) Animals with no hair
b) Animals that eat other animals
c) Animals that have pouches

2. What is a pride?
a) An animal that eats plants
b) A group of lions
c) A mammal

3. What is a panda's favorite food?
a) Grass
b) Bamboo
c) Meat

4. Which animal is nocturnal?
a) Owl
b) Dolphin
c) Giraffe

5. What helps animals hide?
a) Nocturnal
b) Predators
c) Camouflage

6. Which animal is closely related to humans?
a) Cheetah
b) Chimpanzee
c) Gorilla

GLOSSARY

Camouflage: an animal's coloring that helps it hide and blend in

Den: a place for animals to rest in the winter

Herd: a group of animals, such as elephants

Mammals: animals that are warm-blooded, covered in hair, and give birth to live young

Marsupials: mammals with a pouch to carry their young

Nocturnal: awake and active at night

Predators: animals that survive by killing and eating other animals

Pride: a group of lions

Reptiles: animals that are cold-blooded, lay eggs, and are covered in scales

Koala

Elephant

Chimpanzee

Giant Panda

Sea Otter

Giraffe

A baby elephant weighs about 200 pounds at birth! The entire herd of elephants watches over the baby.

A baby koala spends its first six months in its mother's pouch. Once the baby is too big to fi in the pouch, it will ride on its mother's back or cling to her belly!

A baby panda is tiny, only about seven inches long. It won't open its eyes until it is more than a month old.

A baby chimpanzee clings to its mother's fu Then it will ride on its mother's back until it is about two years old.

When a baby giraffe is born, it falls five feet to the ground. But it learns to stand, walk, and run only an hour after birth!

A baby sea otter is born in the water. But the pup will float on its mother's stomach until it is old enough to swim on its own.

HUMAN BODY

Ruth Strother

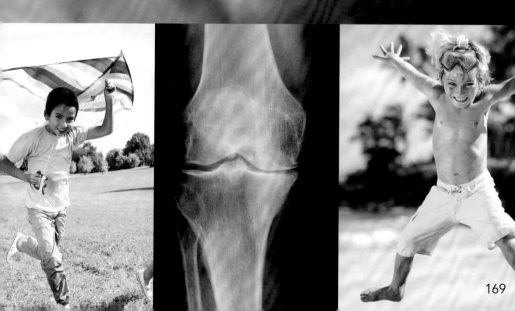

169

CONTENTS

Your Body

Bodies come in all shapes and sizes.
There are animal bodies.
There are insect bodies.
There are human bodies.

Each body is an
amazing machine!

Cells

All living things are made of cells. Cells are so small that you can't see them. Some living things have just one cell. Humans have *trillions* of cells!

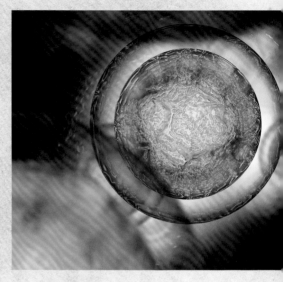

Different cells
have different jobs.
Some cells help
us eat.
Some cells give
our hair, eye, and
skin color.
Some cells attack
germs to keep
us healthy.

Our bodies depend
on cells to live.

Skin, Hair, and Nails

Skin is your biggest body part.
Skin wraps around you and
protects your insides.
Skin gives you the sense of touch.
New skin cells are growing all the time.

Hair grows out of skin.
Skin and hair color come from **melanin**.
Dark hair and skin have a lot of melanin.

Nails grow to protect your fingers and toes. And fingernails come in handy when you have an itch!

Skeleton and Bones

The human skeleton is made of two hundred and six bones. Bones help you move and give you shape.

The spine is made of twenty-six ring-shaped bones called **vertebrae**. You can feel your spine in the center of your back. Those bumps are your vertebrae!

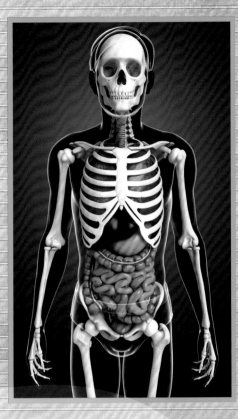

Bones protect your **organs**. Organs are parts of the body that have a job to do. Ribs are bones that protect your lungs and heart. Your skull protects your brain.

A joint is where two bones come together. Joints let you move, bend, and twist.

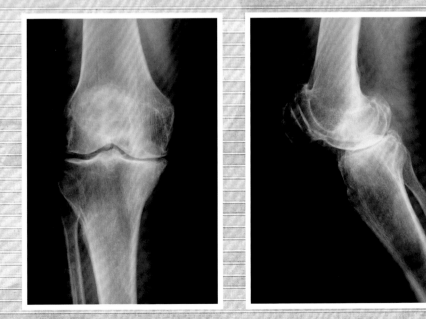

Teeth and Tongue

The human body makes two sets of teeth. Your baby teeth take three years to grow. After a few years, baby teeth are pushed out by adult teeth. Teeth are important for chewing, talking, and singing.

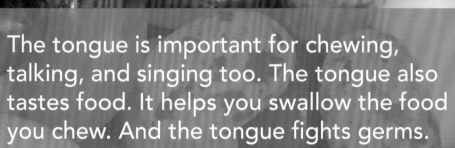

The tongue is important for chewing, talking, and singing too. The tongue also tastes food. It helps you swallow the food you chew. And the tongue fights germs. You can move your tongue because it has a lot of muscles.

Muscles

The human body has about six hundred and fifty muscles. Some muscles are flat and smooth. Smooth muscles work in hollow organs like your stomach. Smooth muscles help push food through your body. Smooth muscles work without your help. You don't even know they are working.

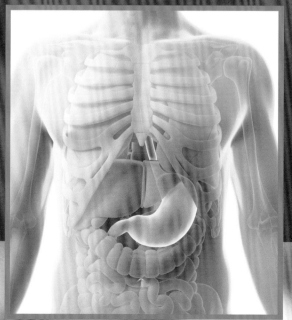

The **cardiac** muscle is your heart. The cardiac muscle pumps blood through your body. This muscle also works on its own.

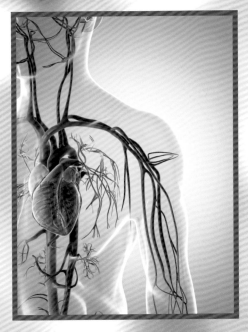

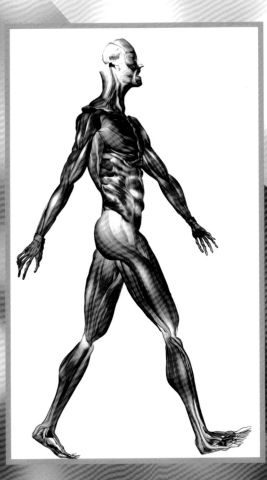

You control your skeletal muscles. Skeletal muscles are connected to your bones. Skeletal muscles form your shape.

Brain and Nerves

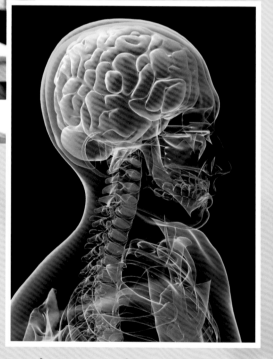

Everything you feel, think, do, and dream starts in your brain. Your brain has billions of tiny cells called **neurons**. Messages from neurons zip around at one hundred and fifty miles per hour. Your brain works faster than a computer!

Messages from the brain travel through nerves in your spine. Nerves branch out from the spine to every part of your body. Nerves send messages back to your brain. Nerves tell your brain about 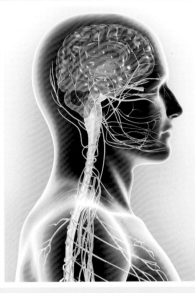 everything. They tell you about what you see, feel, hear, smell, and taste.

Heart and Blood

The heart is a muscle that pumps blood through the body. Blood flows through tubes called **blood vessels**. Blood flows to different parts of the body through arteries. Then blood gets pumped back to the heart through veins.

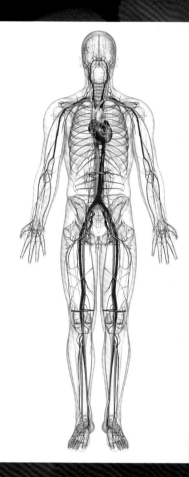

Blood takes oxygen to all the cells in the body. It takes just one minute for blood to reach every cell. The cells use oxygen and make **carbon dioxide**. Blood carries carbon dioxide and other wastes back to the heart. Then the used blood is pumped into the lungs.

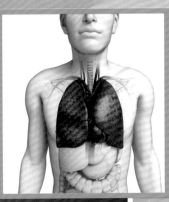

Lungs and Air

Your lungs fill with air every time you breathe in. The air is filled with oxygen. The used blood enters your lungs and picks up oxygen. Then the oxygen-filled blood gets pumped back to the heart.

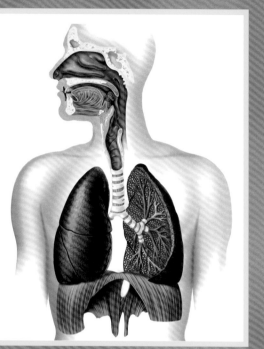

Carbon dioxide and other wastes leave your body when you breathe out.

You have two lungs in your body. The left lung is a bit smaller than the right lung. The left lung is smaller to make room for the heart.

Left

Right

Feeding Your Body

The human body needs food. But not just any food keeps a body healthy. Every day you need to eat from each of the five food groups. Half of the food you eat every day should be fruits and vegetables.

You need to
eat a lot of
grains too.
Wheat, oats, cereals, breads, and pastas are
grains. You need to eat protein such as meat,
beans, and eggs. And dairy like milk and
cheese is important for strong bones.

The Stomach

What happens after you chew and swallow your food?

esophagus

stomach

Muscles push the food down a tube called the **esophagus**. Then the food is stored in the stomach.

The stomach has a lot of acid. The acid and stomach muscles mash the food into smaller soggy pieces. Then the food goes into your small intestine. The food becomes watery and moves into your blood.

small intestine

Getting Rid of Waste

Your blood flows from the small intestines to your liver. The liver decides how much food to store. And it decides how much food to send through the body. The liver also gets rid of waste. Waste goes to your large intestine.

liver

large intestine

small intestine

Kidneys get rid of waste in the blood too. The waste mixes with water. Then the waste is stored in your bladder. You get rid of your waste when you go to the bathroom.

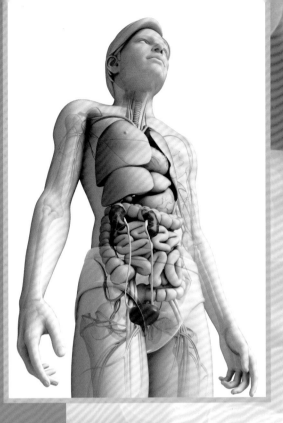

The Five Senses

The human body has five senses.

Your two eyes work together to see what's around you.

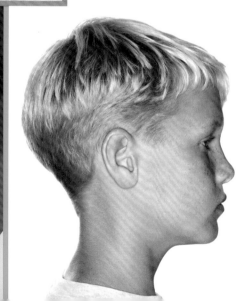

Your ears work together too. They can tell how far away a sound is. They can also tell where the sound is coming from.

Your nose smells everything around you. Your nose also breathes in air.

Your sense of smell helps you taste food. But it's your tongue that does most of the tasting.

Your sense of touch is all over your body. Your sense of touch is in your skin.

195

Keeping Healthy

Keeping your body healthy is very important. Eating healthy foods gives your body the **nutrients** it needs. A healthy body is less likely to get sick.

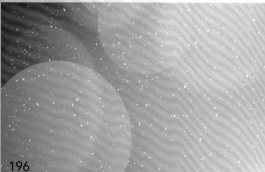

Healthy foods also give you energy. Energy lets you run, play, and exercise. Staying active is important for your body too. Exercise will keep your muscles and heart strong.

HUMAN BODY QUIZ

1. What are all living things made of?
a) Water
b) Cells
c) Oxygen

2. How many bones make up the human skeleton?
a) 206
b) 350
c) 178

3. What do smooth muscles do?
a) Help push food through your body
b) Form your shape
c) Connect to your bones

4. Which is the cardiac muscle?

a) Heart

b) Small intestine

c) Liver

5. What helps the stomach mash food into small pieces?

a) Blood

b) Saliva

c) Acid

6. How many senses does the human body have?

a) Five

b) Seven

c) Three

Answers: 1) b 2) a 3) a 4) a 5) c 6) a

GLOSSARY

Blood vessels: tubes that blood flows through

Carbon dioxide: a gas that we breathe out

Cardiac: anything that relates to the heart

Esophagus: a tube that pushes chewed food from the mouth to the stomach

Melanin: a substance in your body that gives color to your skin, hair, and eyes

Neurons: cells that receive and send signals within the body

Nutrients: substances that are needed for health and growth, such as vitamins, minerals, and proteins

Organs: parts of the body that have a job to do

Vertebrae: the bones that form the spine

LEVEL GUIDELINES

LEVEL 1: EARLY READERS

- Basic factual texts with familiar themes and content
- Concepts in text are reinforced by photos
- Includes glossary to reinforce reading comprehension
- Phonic regularity
- Simple sentence structure and repeated sentence patterns
- Easy vocabulary familiar to kindergarteners and first-graders

LEVEL 2: DEVELOPING READERS

- Simple factual texts with mostly familiar themes and content
- Concepts in text are supported by images
- Includes glossary to reinforce reading comprehension
- Repetition of basic sentence structure with variation of placement of subjects, verbs, and adjectives
- Introduction to new phonic structures
- Integration of contractions, possessives, compound sentences, and some three-syllable words
- Mostly easy vocabulary familiar to kindergarteners and first-graders